A CHILDREN'S FIRST BOOK
ABOUT THEIR ZODIAC SIGN

THE ZODIAC DAUGHTERS

ANTLER & BONE

ISBN: 978-1-966417-40-8 (PRINT)

PUBLISHED BY ANTLER & BONE. ANTLER & BONE'S TITLES MAY BE
PURCHASED IN BULK FOR EDUCATIONAL, BUSINESS, FUNDRAISING, OR
SALES PROMOTIONAL USE. FOR INFORMATION, PLEASE EMAIL
HELLO@ANTLERANDBONE.COM

FIRST PRINT EDITION: 2026

ANTLER & BONE
WWW.ANTLERANDBONE.COM

THIS BOOK BELONGS TO:

_____

(YOUR NAME)

THE ZODIAC DAUGHTERS

High above the sleeping mountains and quiet seas, the stars have always loved to tell stories.

Each night, they gather softly in the sky, watching over the daughters born beneath their light. They notice how every child shines in her own way. Some glow with brave hearts. Some move through the world with gentle hands. Some sparkle with curious minds, while others drift with dreamy imaginations.

Long ago, the stars painted pictures in the sky to celebrate these differences. They shaped animals, symbols, and glowing patterns, each one holding a small story meant just for her. These became the zodiac signs, a tender way to remember that every daughter carries something rare and beautiful within her.

ARIES

BIRTH DATE: MARCH 21ST – APRIL 19TH

Element: Fire | Symbol: The Ram | Ruling Planet: Mars

Daughters born under Aries are often full of energy, courage, and curiosity. They enjoy being first to explore, first to try, and first to help. With warm hearts and bold spirits, they tend to face the world with enthusiasm and confidence.

Primary Colors: Red, Warm Orange, Golden Yellow

Animal: Ram, Falcon, Cheetah

Nature Symbol: Fire, Sunrise, Flame

Flower: Honeysuckle, Tulip

Stone / Crystal: Carnelian, Red Jasper

TAURUS

BIRTH DATE: APRIL 20TH – MAY 20TH

Element: Earth | Symbol: The Bull | Ruling Planet: Venus

Daughters born under Taurus are often gentle, patient, and deeply caring. They enjoy comfort, beauty, and familiar routines, finding joy in simple pleasures and peaceful moments. With steady hearts and calm spirits, they tend to move through the world with quiet strength and loyalty.

Primary Colors: Soft Green, Blush Pink, Earthy Brown

Animal: Bull, Deer, Swan

Nature Symbol: Meadow, Garden, Blooming Earth

Flower: Rose, Poppy

Stone / Crystal: Rose Quartz, Emerald

GEMINI

BIRTH DATE: MAY 21ST – JUNE 20TH

Element: Air | Symbol: The Twins | Ruling Planet: Mercury

Daughters born under Gemini are often curious, expressive, and quick-minded. They enjoy learning, sharing ideas, and exploring many interests at once. With bright minds and playful spirits, they tend to bring joy, conversation, and creativity wherever they go.

Primary Colors: Yellow, Light Blue, Soft Lavender

Animal: Butterfly, Fox, Songbird

Nature Symbol: Breeze, Open Sky, Wind

Flower: Lavender, Lily of the Valley

Stone / Crystal: Citrine, Blue Lace Agate

CANCER

BIRTH DATE: JUNE 21ST – JULY 22ND

Element: Water | Symbol: The Crab | Ruling Planet: The Moon

Daughters born under Cancer are often caring, intuitive, and deeply affectionate. they enjoy nurturing others, creating cozy spaces, and feeling emotionally safe. With tender hearts and gentle spirits, they tend to form strong bonds and offer quiet comfort to those they love.

Primary Colors: Pearl White, Soft Silver, Sea Blue

Animal: Crab, Turtle, Dolphin

Nature Symbol: Moonlight, Tides, Shore

Flower: White Rose, Jasmine

Stone / Crystal: Moonstone, Pearl

LEO

BIRTH DATE: JULY 23RD – AUGUST 22ND

Element: Fire | Symbol: The Lion | Ruling Planet: The Sun

Daughters born under Leo are often warm, confident, and full of joy. They enjoy expressing themselves, being creative, and bringing light into every room. With generous hearts and radiant spirits, they tend to shine through kindness, courage, and natural leadership.

Primary Colors: Gold, Warm Orange, Sun Yellow

Animal: Lion, Peacock, Horse

Nature Symbol: Sun, Light, Flame

Flower: Sunflower, Marigold

Stone / Crystal: Sunstone, Tiger's Eye

VIRGO

BIRTH DATE: AUGUST 23RD — SEPTEMBER 22ND

Element: Earth | Symbol: The Maiden | Ruling Planet: Mercury

Daughters born under Virgo are often thoughtful, gentle, and observant. They enjoy helping others, learning quietly, and creating order in their surroundings. With kind hearts and careful spirits, they tend to show love through patience, service, and attention to detail.

Primary Colors: Sage Green, Soft Beige, Cream

Animal: Dove, Deer, Honeybee

Nature Symbol: Wheat, Meadow, Morning Dew

Flower: Daisy, Morning Glory

Stone / Crystal: Peridot, Amazonite

LIBRA

BIRTH DATE: SEPTEMBER 23ᴿᴰ – OCTOBER 22ᴺᴰ

Element: Air | Symbol: The Scales | Ruling Planet: Venus

Daughters born under Libra are often graceful, kind, and thoughtful. They enjoy harmony, beauty, and peaceful connection with others. With gentle hearts and balanced spirits, they tend to bring fairness, warmth, and calm wherever they go.

Primary Colors: Blush Pink, Sky Blue, Soft Peach

Animal: Swan, Butterfly, Dove

Nature Symbol: Breeze, Open Garden, Balance

Flower: Rose, Hydrangea

Stone / Crystal: Opal, Rose Quartz

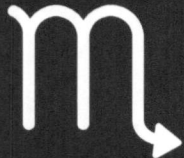

SCORPIO

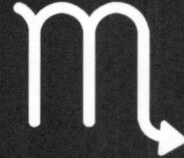

SAGITTARIUS

BIRTH DATE: NOVEMBER 22ND – DECEMBER 21ST

Element: Fire | Symbol: The Archer | Ruling Planet: Jupiter

Daughters born under Sagittarius are often adventurous, optimistic, and free-spirited. They enjoy exploring new places, learning big ideas, and imagining endless possibilities. With joyful hearts and curious spirits, they tend to bring laughter, honesty, and wonder wherever they roam.

Primary Colors: Purple, Royal Blue, Warm Red

Animal: Horse, Owl, Hawk

Nature Symbol: Open Road, Horizon, Flame

Flower: Carnation, Iris

Stone / Crystal: Amethyst, Lapis Lazuli

CAPRICORN

BIRTH DATE: DECEMBER 22ND – JANUARY 19TH

Element: Earth | Symbol: Mountain Goat | Ruling Planet: Saturn

Daughters born under Capricorn are often thoughtful, determined, and wise beyond their years. They enjoy learning, building, and working toward meaningful goals. With steady hearts and patient spirits, they tend to move through the world with quiet confidence, responsibility, and strength.

Primary Colors: Forest Green, Charcoal Gray, Soft Brown

Animal: Mountain Goat, Bear, Wolf

Nature Symbol: Mountain, Stone, Winter Sky

Flower: Pansy, Snowdrop

Stone / Crystal: Garnet, Onyx

AQUARIUS

BIRTH DATE: JANUARY 20TH – FEBRUARY 18TH

Element: Air | Symbol: The Water Bearer | Ruling Planet: Uranus

Daughters born under Aquarius are often imaginative, thoughtful, and independent. They enjoy new ideas, creative expression, and seeing the world in unique ways. With open hearts and visionary spirits, they tend to bring originality, kindness, and curiosity wherever they go.

Primary Colors: Turquoise, Sky Blue, Silver

Animal: Dolphin, Owl, Butterfly

Nature Symbol: Wind, Stars, Flowing Water

Flower: Orchid, Blue Violet

Stone / Crystal: Amethyst, Aquamarine

PISCES

BIRTH DATE: FEBRUARY 19ᵀᴴ – MARCH 20ᵀᴴ

Element: Water | Symbol: The Fish | Ruling Planet: Neptune

Daughters born under Pisces are often gentle, imaginative, and deeply caring. They enjoy creativity, storytelling, and moments of quiet reflection. With compassionate hearts and dreamy spirits, they tend to move through the world with kindness, empathy, and emotional depth.

Primary Colors: Sea Green, Lavender, Soft Blue
Animal: Fish, Seahorse, Deer
Nature Symbol: Ocean, Mist, Moonlight
Flower: Water Lily, Lotus
Stone / Crystal: Aquamarine, Amethyst

SHOP MORE BOOKS AT

WWW.ANTLERANDBONE.COM

www.ingramcontent.com/pod-product-compliance
Lightning Source LLC
Chambersburg PA
CBHW060839270326
41933CB00002B/133